Jonah

God's Grace for Everyone

By Clay Gentry

Published by
Spiritbuilding Publishers
9700 Ferry Road, Waynesville, Ohio 45068

JONAH: GOD'S GRACE FOR EVERYONE
By Clay Gentry

ISBN: 978–1–964–80519–1

Spiritbuilding
PUBLISHERS

spiritbuilding.com

Table of Contents

Introduction

Dive into the depths of Jonah's extraordinary adventure, a tale that transcends the familiar Sunday school narrative and invites us to confront the depths of our own hearts. Unravel the layers of this captivating narrative, filled with rebellion, repentance, and the surprising grace of God.

Together, we'll navigate the tumultuous waters of Jonah's story, exploring the complexities of his resistance, the surprising repentance of Nineveh, and the profound lessons that echo through the ages—all the way to the shores of the New Testament, where we'll encounter Jonah in Jesus' resurrection, the salvation of the Gentiles, and even Paul's dramatic voyage to Rome. As you immerse yourself in the Bible, let the ancient words resonate in you, sparking introspection, igniting conversations, and guiding you toward a deeper understanding of God's amazing grace and unwavering purpose.

This study guide is more than just an intellectual exercise; it's an invitation to encounter the living God, the God who pursues us even in our darkest moments, the God who calls us to be agents of His grace and heralds of His transformative power.

Here's how our journey will unfold:

- **Immerse:** Begin by reading the designated passages from the book of Jonah and the New Testament, meditating on the words and allowing them to speak to your heart.
- **Reflect:** Engage with thought-provoking questions designed to spark self-examination and challenge your perspectives. Delve into Jonah's experience and discover how his struggles mirror your own.
- **Respond:** Conclude each lesson with a prayer prompt, an invitation to pour out your heart to God, seeking His guidance, His forgiveness, and the power of His grace in your life.

As we embark on this study together, may our hearts be open to the lessons that await us, and may our lives be changed by our encounter with God's word.

Lesson 1

Jonah: More Than a Fish Story

The story of a "great fish" swallowing Jonah is etched into the collective memory of every person brought up in the church. We may think we know it well, but this narrative is far more than a children's felt board story—it's a profound exploration of human nature, divine grace, and the challenge of obedience. Yet, in our hearts, each of us is like Jonah: We rebel against God's commands. We resist compassion and grace. We remain distant from the God we claim to serve and the people He wants to save. Everyone in Jonah's story is in desperate need of heaven's mercy—Jonah, the sailors, the Ninevites, and you.

Before we delve into its depths, take a moment to immerse yourself in the book of Jonah. Read all four chapters, allowing the ancient words to resonate in your heart.

Facing Our Inner Jonah

Now, let's embark on a journey beyond the familiar:

1. **Past Impressions:** What have been your past impressions of Jonah's story?

2. **More Than a Fish Story:** While the "great fish" dominates most recollections, what other significant themes emerge from the narrative? What truths resonate with your own experiences?

3. **The Heart of the Matter:** If you had to distill the essence of Jonah's message into a single, powerful statement, what would it be?

4. **A Personal Call:** Imagine God calling you to a place that fills you with dread. Where would that be? What makes it so daunting? What would your initial response be?

5. **Reflecting on Jonah:** Look carefully at Jonah's story, do any of his behaviors or reactions stir something within you? Do you recognize any of your struggles in his journey? Explain.

6. **Learning from Jonah:** As you begin your journey with Jonah, identify several lessons you want to learn. For example: loving God and your neighbor, evangelism, grace, judgment, etc.

A Journey of Transformation

Jonah's story is an odyssey of transformation, a reluctant embrace of God's boundless grace. It's a story that continues to echo in our lives today. As you reflect on Jonah's struggles and eventual surrender, remember that his journey is also our own. May we learn from his mistakes, open our hearts to God's compassion, and boldly share His love with a world in need.

Prayer Prompt: Lord, as I begin to study Jonah, open my mind and heart to Your truth. Show me something new in this familiar story and how it speaks to my life today.

Lesson 2

Running from God

The book of Jonah opens with a familiar prophetic rhythm: "The word of the Lord came to Jonah" (v. 1). Yet, this seemingly ordinary beginning quickly veers into uncharted territory, "Arise, go to Nineveh…" God's directive to Jonah is to pronounce judgment upon Nineveh, the notorious capital of the brutal Assyrian empire, Israel's sworn enemy. While other prophets had declared God's judgment upon Israel's enemies (cf. Amos 1:1—2:3), none were ever sent directly to the heart of the enemy's power. This command proves too much for Jonah, leading him to rebel and flee. But the question remains: why?

Before we journey further into Jonah's rebellion, let's ground ourselves in the opening verses of this captivating narrative (Jonah 1:1–3).

Unveiling the Depths of Disobedience

Now, let's explore the layers of meaning woven into Jonah's flight from grace:

1. **The Face of Brutality:** History paints a grim picture of the Assyrians, renowned for their ruthlessness and cruelty, particularly toward those they conquered. Delve into the annals of history (via Google) and uncover the depths of their brutality. Share your findings with the class, painting a vivid picture of the people Jonah was called to confront.

2. **A Prophet's Past:** We first encounter Jonah in 2 Kings 14:23–27, during a period of relative peace before Assyria's iron fist tightens its grip on Israel (cf. 2 Kings 15:19–20; 17:1–41). Revisit this passage and summarize Jonah's role in this episode. Why do you think Jonah has no problem prophesying to the wicked, idolatrous king of Israel, but not the Ninevites?

3. **A Divine Paradox:** Why do you think God sends Jonah, a prophet of Israel, to Nineveh? What message is God sending to both Israel and Assyria?

4. **A Desperate Escape:** Instead of journeying eastward toward Nineveh, Jonah boards a ship bound for Tarshish, the westernmost edge of the known world, seeking to "flee from the presence of the Lord." What do you imagine Jonah is hoping to achieve through this desperate act of defiance?

5. **A Deeper Rebellion:** Later in the narrative, Jonah 4:1–3 reveals the prophet's true motive for running. Do you sense Jonah's rebellion goes beyond merely refusing a divine assignment? Is there a deeper struggle with the very nature and character of God? Explain your thinking.

6. **The Impossibility of Escape:** Jonah's attempt to flee God's presence seems foolish, but haven't we all tried to outrun God at some point? Reflect on the profound truth and comfort of Psalm 139:1–12. In what ways do you sometimes live as if you can escape God's all-seeing eye and sovereign hand?

Confronting Our Own Rebellion

Jonah's initial response to God's call exposes a struggle that resides within each of us: the temptation to flee from challenges, especially those that disrupt our comforts, and lead us into unfamiliar territory—both physically and emotionally. His flight to Tarshish underscores the futility of attempting to escape God's call and the inevitable consequences of disobedience. By delving into Jonah's motives and actions in these first few verses, we've gained a deeper understanding of our tendencies to resist God's will and the transformative power of surrendering to His plan, even when it involves venturing into the unknown or confronting our fears.

Prayer Prompt: Lord, forgive me when I, like Jonah, try to run from Your presence and purpose for my life. Create in me a willing heart and the courage to obey your commands.

Lesson 3

When God Hurls a Storm

Wat becomes of the wicked? Some say lock them up, write them off, and proverbially "throw away the key." The book of Jonah grapples with this very question, albeit in a manner that defies our expectations. Jonah, God's prophet, attempts to flee his divine mandate, but God, in a display of steadfast love, unleashes His divine power, "The LORD hurled a great wind upon the sea" (v. 4). The word "hurled" evokes the image of a weapon such as a spear launched with precision and force (cf. 1 Samuel 18:11), a vivid metaphor for the tempest God directs toward Jonah's vessel. If the prophet refuses to journey to the great city of Nineveh, then he will go headlong into the heart of a raging storm.

Before we navigate the depths of this tempestuous encounter, let's immerse ourselves in the dramatic events of Jonah 1:4–16.

Adrift in a Sea of Disobedience

Now, let's explore the nuances of this divine intervention and its impact on Jonah and those caught in his wake:

1. **A Contrasting Response:** Imagine yourself among the terrified sailors on that storm-tossed ship. Contrast their frantic response to the impending peril with Jonah's seemingly serene indifference. What, if anything, does this reveal about their respective states of mind and perspectives?

2. **A Captain's Rebuke:** Step into the sandals of the ship's captain and rephrase his exasperated admonishment to Jonah. Why do you think Jonah shows little concern for the sailors, even though his actions are endangering their lives?

3. **Jonah Unmasked:** In their desperation, the sailors cast lots to determine blame, and the lot falls upon Jonah (cf. Proverbs 16:33). Observe how he identifies himself when confronted. What significance, if any, do you find in his self-proclamation? How have Jonah's actions either aligned with or betrayed his own identity?

4. **A Glimmer of Change?:** Evaluate Jonah's proposal to quell the storm. Do you detect a shift in his demeanor or attitude? What's motivating his suggestion?

5. **Unexpected Piety:** By the end of this turbulent scene, the Gentile sailors "feared the LORD exceedingly." In what ways do the pagan sailors demonstrate a more profound understanding of reverence and repentance than Jonah? When have you seen similar instances where those outside the faith exhibit greater spiritual awareness than those within (including you)?

6. **A Shared Humanity:** In what ways does the storm-tossed vessel serve as a metaphor for the shared human experience? In what ways can you actively seek the common good of your neighbor, regardless of their beliefs or background? Identify practical steps to guard against the insidious danger of graceless indifference toward others.

The Tempest Within

The storm that engulfs Jonah serves as a stark reminder that we cannot evade the consequences of our disobedience, no matter how far we flee. It also exposes the stark contrast between Jonah's apathy and the sailors' desperate cries for deliverance, while underscoring the profound impact our actions can have on those around us. Ultimately, this episode compels us to examine our responses to adversity and consider how our faith and obedience, or lack thereof, shape our interactions with both believers and non-believers. Are we willing to acknowledge our role in the "storms" of life and actively contribute to the well-being of others, or do we remain indifferent to the needs of those around us?

Prayer Prompt: Lord, reveal to me where I'm running from You. Show me how my disobedience impacts those around me, even in ways I may not see. Give me the strength to turn back to You and take responsibility for my choices.

Lesson 4

A Cry from the Abyss

As the sailors toss Jonah overboard and tempest-tossed waves crash over Jonah, one might imagine him resigned to his fate, relieved even, that his mission to Nineveh was thwarted. Yet, throughout Jonah's desperate flight, God's sovereign hand orchestrates a divine intervention. Defiant and ready to perish rather than relent, Jonah finds himself swallowed whole by a "great fish" sent by the very God he sought to avoid. It is here, in the belly of the beast, enveloped in darkness and isolation of the abyss, that Jonah must confront his rebellious spirit in the crucible of the loving grace of His God.

Before we descend into the abyss of Jonah's despair and redemption, let's listen closely to the poignant prayer of Jonah 1:17—2:10.

Confined by Grace

Now, let's explore the depths of this transformative encounter:

1. **Captivated by the Creature:** The image of Jonah swallowed by the "great fish" has captivated imaginations for centuries. Why do you think this aspect of the story overshadows other crucial elements? How might a fixation on this one scene detract from a broad understanding of Jonah's overall message?

2. **The Crucible of Grace:** The "great fish" is more than a fantastical element in a children's story; it functions as an instrument of

God's grace and a crucible of refinement. Reflect on the themes of discipline and spiritual growth in Hebrews 12:3–17. How does Jonah's confinement within the fish parallel the refining fire of God's corrective love?

3. **A Belated Plea:** Ironically, the prophet who sought to escape God's presence now cries out to Him from the depths of his despair. Why do you think Jonah waits until this moment of utter hopelessness to pray and make vows (as opposed to not praying during the storm 1:6)? What does this say about the human tendency to seek God only during a perceived crisis?

4. **A Cry from the Abyss:** From the belly of the fish, Jonah offers a highly theological prayer infused with quotes from the Psalms, expressions of thanksgiving, with references to God, the temple, sacrifices and vows but devoid of confession and/or repentance. What strikes you about his prayer? Do you sense any irony in his words verses his past and future actions? Like Jonah, can you pray a good prayer but struggle to faithfully apply your words? Explain.

5. **The Irony of Grace:** Compare vv. 7, 9 of Jonah's prayer with his reasons for fleeing as stated in Jonah 4:1–3. How do his perspectives on God's grace differ when he is the recipient, rather than the people of Nineveh? What does this reveal about the human struggle to extend the same grace to others that we readily suppose for ourselves?

6. **Unwavering Faithfulness:** Why does God demonstrate such steadfast love and faithfulness to a rebellious prophet like Jonah—or us, for that matter? What does this disclose about the unwavering nature of God's love and His relentless pursuit of His wayward children?

A Journey of Reluctant Surrender

Jonah's experience in the belly of the fish, though often relegated to a children's Bible class, represents a profound encounter with God's loving grace. This period of isolation and introspection serves as a turning point in Jonah's narrative, forcing him to confront his disobedience and ultimately leading him back to a place of surrender. By exploring the symbolism of the fish as an instrument of grace and divine discipline, along with the complexities of Jonah's prayer from the depths, we can gain a deeper appreciation for the lengths to which God will go to restore His rebellious children.

Prayer Prompt: Lord, like Jonah, I confess I run from Your will. Show me where I'm seeking to escape Your purpose and help me embrace the discipline of Your grace, leading me to surrender and obedience.

Lesson 5

Preaching Judgment and Grace

A stonishingly, God's voice reverberates again, extending a second chance to the undeserving prophet. Jonah, harboring resentment and a lingering aversion to his mission, is summoned anew to the city he loathes. "Arise, go to Nineveh, that great city, and call out against it the message that I tell you" (Jonah 3:1–2). God, in His unwavering steadfastness, places Jonah back at the precious point of his previous failure, confronting him with the very task he so desperately sought to evade—preach God's judgment. But it's Jonah's narrow view of grace that creates a deep internal conflict, preventing him from preaching to his enemies, even though he has been forgiven. Yet, God's grace transcends the boundaries of human labels, embracing all of creation—the rebellious prophet, the infamous city, and each of us, regardless of our perceived worthiness.

Before we join Jonah on his reluctant return to Nineveh, let's hear the LORD's directive in Jonah 3:1–5.

A Second Chance to Preach God's Judgment and Grace

Now, let's explore the nuances of this second call and the lessons it holds for us:

1. **A Divine Portrait:** The LORD, in His infinite patience, grants Jonah another opportunity to obey, reiterating His command to journey to Nineveh. How does this second-chance illustrate Jonah's description of God in Jonah 4:2 (cf. 1 Timothy 1:12–17)? What does it reveal

about the character of God, that He extends grace even to those who defy Him?

2. **A Shift in Focus:** Compare Jonah's initial call in Jonah 1:1–3 with this renewed summons in Jonah 3:1–3. Why do you think God subtly shifts the emphasis from Nineveh's wickedness to His role as the orchestrator of Jonah's message?

3. **A Concise Proclamation:** "Yet forty days, and Nineveh shall be overthrown!" (Jonah 3:4) constitutes the entirety of Jonah's recorded message. Do you interpret this as the complete content, or a mere summary of his inspired proclamation? Elaborate.

4. **A Transformed Messenger?:** As you envision Jonah traversing the streets of Nineveh and proclaiming its coming destruction, how do you picture his interactions with the Ninevites? Do you see his experience with the "great fish" softened his heart or hardened his resolve?

5. **The Intertwined Nature of Grace and Judgment:** It's tempting to present God's judgment and grace as separate entities, but they are inextricably linked. Why is it essential that preaching on judgment incorporates the reality of grace, and vice versa? How do these two aspects of God's character—"kindness and severity" (Rom 11:22a)—complement and illuminate each other?

6. **A Balanced Message:** Based on your understanding of the gospel, do you tend to emphasize judgment or grace more prominently? How can you cultivate a more balanced perspective, becoming a messenger who faithfully communicates both the justice and love of God?

Embracing the Grace and Judgment of God

Jonah's second call to Nineveh underscores the patient and persistent nature of God, who extends renewed opportunities even after we stumble and fall. This lesson invites us to reflect on how God's commands, though often challenging and even seemingly contradictory, ultimately serve His redemptive purposes. By pondering Jonah's message and the potential impact of his own experience with grace, we can glean valuable insights into communicating God's truth with both conviction and compassion. Furthermore, exploring the delicate balance between grace and judgment allows us to evaluate our approach to sharing the Gospel and mature as more effective heralds of God's love and justice.

Prayer Prompt: Lord, help me to be a faithful messenger of Your Word, communicating Your judgment and Your grace with clarity and compassion. Soften my heart toward those who are different from me or whom I consider undeserving and empower me to extend Your love to all.

Lesson 6

An Unexpected Repentance

The collective repentance that sweeps through Nineveh is arguably the most astonishing event in the book of Jonah, far surpassing the miracle of the "great fish" in its profound implications. The Assyrians, infamous throughout the ancient world for their ruthlessness and disregard for human life, stand as a stark contrast to the image of humble penitence. Yet, these hardened people, renowned for their brutality, uniquely respond to the prophet's message, repenting in a manner that reverberates through their entire society, "from the greatest of them to the least of them." Their transformation is so complete that it even includes their livestock in their collective act of contrition. Through Jonah's terse proclamation of judgment, the Ninevites find redemption, and God, in His infinite mercy, relents from His intended destruction—precisely the outcome Jonah dreaded.

Before we delve into the depths of this unexpected transformation, let's witness the remarkable account in Jonah 3:6–10.

Embracing the Unthinkable

Now, let's explore the multifaceted dimensions of this extraordinary repentance:

1. **A City Transformed:** Catalog the various ways the Ninevites, from their king to the lowest slave, express their remorse and seek God's favor. What aspects of their overwhelming repentance resonate most powerfully with you?

2. **The Power of Proclamation:** The Ninevites' enthusiastic response, despite Jonah's reluctant delivery, speaks volumes about God's ability to draw people to Himself, regardless of the messenger's shortcomings. How does this empower you to proclaim God's word to others, even when facing apathy or resistance?

3. **A Model of Repentance:** The Ninevites repent, not knowing if God would spare their city or not, "Who knows?" the king decrees, "God may turn and relent…" (v. 9). Evaluate the king's words. In what ways does genuine remorse for our transgressions motivate us to repent, no matter the outcome (cf. Joel 2:12–14)?

4. **A Relenting God:** Jonah 3:10 is a pivotal verse that reveals God's compassionate response to the Ninevites' repentance. He spares the city, demonstrating His unwavering desire for the redemption of all humanity. How does this challenge your understanding of God's justice and grace?

5. **Overcoming Doubt:** The Ninevites' response, given their reputation, may seem surprising, even improbable. Yet shouldn't we expect that God can work in any heart, regardless of its past? Reflect on instances where doubt or preconceived notions about others have hindered you from sharing the Gospel.

6. **A New Song of Repentance:** Embrace your creativity and compose new lyrics to the familiar tune of "Who Did Swallow Jonah?" that capture the essence of the Ninevites' remarkable repentance. Introduce it to the children's classes at your congregation.

Beyond the Expected

The Ninevites' response to Jonah's preaching underscores the transformative power of repentance, even in the most unexpected circumstances. Despite their history of brutality, their wholehearted embracing of God's message demonstrates that no one is beyond the reach of divine grace. This lesson challenges us to dismantle our preconceived notions about who is "worthy" of God's love, and empowers us to share the Gospel boldly, trusting that the Word can work in even the most hardened hearts. The Ninevites' example serves as a powerful reminder that repentance leads to transformed lives and that God desires the salvation of all people, regardless of their past.

Prayer Prompt: Lord, forgive me for the times I have judged others as unworthy of Your love or beyond the reach of Your grace. Your Word is powerful and effective, capable of transforming even the hardest hearts. Help me to never underestimate the impact of Your gospel and to proclaim it to the world boldly.

Lesson 7

The Bitter Root of Resentment

The repentance of Nineveh, a cause for universal rejoicing, ignites a firestorm of fury within Jonah. He retreats to a vantage point outside the city, stewing in a cauldron of bitterness and resentment. Despite experiencing God's grace firsthand in the belly of the fish and demonstrating a flicker of obedience, Jonah's heart remains stubbornly resistant to the boundless grace he has witnessed. His initial flight from God stemmed from a deep-seated aversion to the very nature of divine mercy, a refusal to accept God as He truly is. Jonah, cloaked in an outward veneer of righteousness, harbors a heart consumed by a darkness that mirrors the wickedness he condemns in others—and, not surprisingly, within each of us lies the potential for a similar struggle.

Before confronting the shadows within our hearts, let's observe Jonah's embittered response in Jonah 4:1–3.

Wrestling with the God of Grace

Now, let's navigate the turbulent waters of Jonah's anger and its implications for our spiritual journeys:

1. **A Tale of Two Prayers:** Jonah's fury at God's gracious forgiveness of Nineveh prompts his second prayer in the book. Compare this prayer with his earlier plea for deliverance in Jonah 2:1–9. What significant shifts in tone, focus, and attitude do you observe?

2. **Jonah's Expectations:** What are Jonah's expectations for God's grace? How does his attitude change when God directs His mercy toward Nineveh rather than Jonah or Israel?

3. **Echoes of Sinai:** For his prayer, Jonah hurls God's words back at Him, quoting from Exodus 34:6–7. Recall the context in which God originally spoke these words. What was the significance of this divine self-revelation at that moment in Israel's history?

4. **A Misguided Appeal to Scripture:** How does Jonah twist Scripture to justify his indignation, anger, and bitterness? Do you believe his outburst stems from a misunderstanding or a willful rejection of God's character? Explain your perspective.

5. **Our Personal Nineveh:** Do you have your own "Nineveh," a person or group of people you struggle with extending grace to? Who are they, and why do you believe they are undeserving of God's mercy and forgiveness? What does this reveal about your understanding of grace and the human capacity for change?

6. **Reflecting the Divine Image:** Scripture repeatedly calls Christians to emulate the character of God (Luke 6:27–36; Ephesians 4:32–5:2; 1 Peter 1:15–16; 1 John 4:11). Identify practical ways you can actively reflect God's mercy and forgiveness toward your "Nineveh," extending grace even when it is or feels undeserved.

The Unsettling Mirror of Grace

Jonah's anger at God's mercy towards Nineveh exposes a common human struggle: our tendency to cling to judgment and resentment, even when forgiveness triumphs. This lesson challenges us to confront the darkness that lurks within our hearts, questioning whether we genuinely comprehend and embrace the boundless compassion of God. By analyzing Jonah's reaction and reflecting on our experiences with forgiveness, we can identify the roots of our resistance to grace and actively cultivate a heart that mirrors God's love and mercy towards all.

Prayer Prompt: Lord, deepen my understanding of Your boundless grace and help me to extend it freely to others, even those I deem undeserving. Transform my heart to reflect Your compassion and break down any barriers of prejudice or judgment that prevent me from loving others as You love them.

Lesson 8

God's Grace for Everyone

W hile righteous anger has its place, as exemplified by Jesus' response to the hypocrisy He encountered (cf. Mark 3:5), much of our anger stems from a misaligned perspective. Anger, like a blinding fog, distorts our perception of truth (even God's word) and twists our thinking, as vividly illustrated by Jonah's experience. Worse yet, anger erects barriers to grace and compassion. God, in His infinite wisdom, confronts Jonah's fury, inviting him—and us—to examine the legitimacy of our anger. The narrative concludes abruptly, leaving us with a poignant question reverberating through the ages. Will we embrace the splendor of a gracious God, reflecting His boundless compassion for everyone? Or will we succumb to the consuming flames of indignation, separating ourselves from others, and ultimately from the gracious God we so desperately need?

Before we grapple with these profound questions, let's engage with the final verses of Jonah's narrative (Jonah 4:4–11).

A Confrontation of Compassion

Now, let's explore the depths of this divine dialogue and its implications for our spiritual formation:

1. **Unmerited Mercy:** Jonah's previous act of disobedience landed him in a raging tempest. What consequences might we anticipate for this renewed rebellion? Instead, how does God, again, extend mercy to His headstrong prophet? What does this reveal about the inexhaustible nature of His grace?

2. **The Purpose of Inquiry:** God confronts Jonah with a penetrating question: "Do you do well to be angry?" (Jonah 4:4). Reflect on God's purpose in posing this question (cf. Genesis 4:6–7). What is the significance of Jonah's unrestrained fury? How should he respond to this divine question?

3. **A Reminder of Grace:** Outside the city walls, Jonah constructs a makeshift "booth," a structure reminiscent of Israel's sacred festivals—the Feast of Booths. What spiritual significance did these booths hold for the Israelites (Leviticus 23:33–44)? In what ways should this symbolic act remind Jonah of God's grace and provision for a rebellious people?

4. **The Transformative Feast:** Consider the Lord's Supper, the sole religious feast the New Testament prescribes. In what ways should this weekly remembrance of God's sacrificial love and grace shape our understanding of Him, ourselves, and everyone else?

5. **An Unanswered Question:** The book of Jonah concludes with an open-ended question: "Should I not pity Nineveh…who do not know their right hand from their left, and also much cattle?" (Jonah 4:11). Why do you think the narrative abruptly ends on this unresolved note? What is the implicit answer God seeks from Jonah and you?

6. **A Call to Action:** Reflect on how your study of Jonah has inspired you to boldly proclaim both God's judgment and His grace, particularly to those who seem undeserving or different than you. How can you actively participate in God's mission to bring the lost to repentance?

Beyond Human Limitations

Jonah's story culminates not with a triumphant declaration of obedience but with an open-ended question, compelling us to confront our capacity for compassion and our discomfort with God's boundless mercy. This lesson invites us to reflect on the nature of genuine repentance and the transformative power of grace, even for those we deem undeserving. By contemplating God's patient interaction with Jonah and His concern for all creation, we can learn to align our perspectives with His, embracing a broader understanding of love and justice that extends to everyone.

Prayer Prompt: Lord, like Jonah, I confess that my anger sometimes clouds my judgment and hinders my compassion. Soften my heart toward those who have hurt me or those I struggle to understand. Help me to see their humanity and need for Your grace.

Nahum:
Day Forty-One and Beyond

The dramatic repentance of Nineveh under Jonah's preaching leaves a lingering question: Was this transformation genuine and lasting, or merely a fleeting response to imminent danger? Nahum, a century later, provides a sobering answer. His prophecy paints a stark picture of a city that has abandoned its remorse, reverting to the violence and oppression that once defined it. This stark contrast compels us to confront the fragility of our commitments. Do we, like the Ninevites, allow our radical repentance to fade away when the crisis passes? Do we succumb to the subtle erosion of complacency, compromising our resolve to follow God wholeheartedly no matter what?

Before we explore the applications of Nahum's message, let's consider his searing prophecy (Nahum 1:1–3:19).

The Unraveling of Repentance

Now, let's explore the implications of Nineveh's relapse and its relevance for our spiritual journeys:

1. **A Fleeting Transformation:** Imagine the forty-first day after Jonah preached his message of judgment (Jonah 3:4–5). How do you envision the Ninevites conducting themselves? Did they doubt God was ever going to destroy them? How long do you think they embraced their new grace-trained life? Or do you sense something else?

2. **A Return to Darkness:** Despite their earlier unconditional contrition, Nahum exposes a resurgence of sin and injustice within Nineveh. What specific transgressions does he identify? How does this reveal the deceptive nature of fleeting repentance?

3. **Contrasting Portraits:** We've seen God's compassion in Jonah, but Nahum paints a picture of a God of justice and wrath. How do these two prophetic voices complement each other in presenting a holistic picture of God?

4. **The Nineveh Within:** We all harbor a "Nineveh" within ourselves—areas of our lives where we are prone to regress, old habits stubbornly persist, and our values are readily compromised. How can we honestly identify these inner strongholds of sin?

5. **A Prophetic Wake-Up Call:** Nahum's message warns against complacency, reminding us that unrepentant sin carries dire consequences. How can we allow Nahum's prophetic voice to shake us from spiritual slumber and reignite our commitment to wholehearted discipleship?

6. **Balancing Grace and Severity:** How can we effectively balance the urgency of Nahum's message with the grace exemplified in Jonah's story? In what ways do we avoid minimizing the gravity of sin while upholding the hope of redemption?

The Enduring Journey of Transformation

Let us not merely observe the historical downfall of Nineveh but internalize the lessons it holds for our own lives. The Ninevites, despite their zealous repentance under Jonah's preaching, ultimately succumbed to the allure of their former ways, demonstrating the precarious nature of faith without ongoing commitment. We, too, must actively guard against complacency, cultivating a heart trained by God's grace that resists the pull of old patterns. May Nahum's message serves as a constant reminder to remain vigilant, deepen our repentance, and walk steadfastly in the light of God's truth, ensuring that our transformation is not a fleeting moment but an enduring journey toward lasting change.

Prayer Prompt: Lord, I confess that my repentance, like that of the Ninevites, can sometimes be temporary. Forgive me for the times I have turned away from You after experiencing Your grace. I pray for a heart that clings to You not just in times of crisis, but in every moment of my life.

Lesson 10

The Sign of Jonah: A Foreshadowing of Resurrection

T he Scriptures, in their entirety, bear witness to Jesus (cf. Luke 24:27). While we often link Him primarily to the New Testament, a closer look reveals His presence woven throughout the Old Testament narratives as well. Every flawed hero, every imperfect prophet, anticipates the arrival of the ultimate Savior. Even Jonah, the reluctant prophet who fled from God's call, unexpectedly directs our attention toward Jesus. When Jesus engages in a tense exchange with the religious leaders of His day, they demand a sign—a miraculous display to confirm His authority. His response? He points them back to the story of Jonah, a seemingly obscure tale of a prophet swallowed by a giant fish. However, within this unlikely narrative lies a profound foreshadowing of Jesus' death and resurrection, a "sign" that reveals the heart of God's redemptive plan.

Before we explore this profound connection, let's read the exchange between Jesus and the religious leaders in Matthew 12:38–41; 16:1–4.

Unveiling the True Sign

Now, let's delve into the significance of Jonah's sign and its fulfillment in Christ:

1. **A Tale of Two Callings:** Compare Jonah's commission to Nineveh with Jesus' incarnation on Earth (see Philippians 2:1–11). How does Jesus, in His perfect obedience and unwavering compassion, surpass Jonah as the embodiment of God's redemptive mission?

2. **A Demand for Proof:** What motivates the Scribes and Pharisees to demand a sign from Jesus? Why does their request elicit such a strong rebuke?

3. **Jonah as a Precursor:** Instead of acquiescing to their demands, Jesus points His detractors back to the account of Jonah. How does Jonah's self-sacrifice and his time in the fish foreshadow Jesus' death, burial, and resurrection?

4. **Ninevah as Judge:** How was Ninevah saved from judgment? By implication, how did Jesus suggest His own audience could be saved? Why would Ninevah—a city of Gentiles—stand in judgment against Jesus' Jewish detractors?

5. **The Disciples' Blindness:** Despite Jesus' repeated predictions of His death and resurrection (cf. Matthew 16:21; 17:22–23; 20:17–19), even with Jonah's experience as a backdrop, why did the disciples struggle to grasp this fundamental truth?

6. **Contesting the Resurrection:** Matthew's Gospel uniquely records the authorities' attempts to suppress the truth of Jesus' resurrection (Matthew 27:62–66; 28:11–15). Research some contemporary arguments against the resurrection. How do these challenges echo the skepticism and resistance Jesus and His followers encountered (cf. Acts 17:32a; 26:8)?

7. **The Cornerstone of Faith:** The resurrection of Jesus is the bedrock of Christian belief (1 Corinthians 15:14). Compile a long list of passages highlighting the resurrection's power and significance for believers. Share how this exercise has strengthened your faith in Jesus and His victory over death.

Embracing the Hope of Resurrection

As we conclude our exploration of Jonah's sign and its profound connection to Jesus, let's remember that the entire biblical narrative ultimately points to Christ. Just as Jonah sacrificed himself for others, and emerged from the depths of the great fish, foreshadowing Jesus' death and triumphant resurrection, we too can find hope and new life in Christ's victory over death. The resurrection is the cornerstone of our faith, a testament to God's power and love that shatters the darkness of sin and death. By embracing this truth, we can walk in the light of His grace, empowered to live lives of purpose and joy, sharing the message of salvation with a world in desperate need of hope.

Prayer Prompt: Lord, open my eyes to see Jesus in all Scripture, even in Old Testament accounts like Jonah's. Help me understand how every page of Scripture points to You and Your redemptive plan.

The Sign of Jonah:
A Prelude to Gentile Inclusion

The Gospels, while harmonious in their portrayal of Jesus, offer unique lenses through which to view His ministry. Luke, uniquely presents a compelling twist on "The Sign of Jonah." While Matthew emphasizes the physical resurrection, Luke subtly shifts the focus to something quite unexpected and controversial: the repentance of the Gentiles. Just as God showed mercy to the Gentile city of Nineveh in the book of Jonah, so too would He extend His grace to all nations through Jesus. This subtle shift not only enriches our understanding of Jesus' ministry but also foreshadows the groundbreaking expansion of the Gospel's reach, a theme that takes center stage in the book of Acts.

Before we explore this unique Lukan perspective, let's listen in as Jesus teaches the crowds in Luke 11:29–32.

Expanding the Scope of Salvation

Now, let's delve into the significance of Luke's portrayal of "The Sign of Jonah":

1. **A Wicked Demand:** Beginning with v. 16, we witness the crowd clamoring for a sign from Jesus to validate His messianic claims. Why does Jesus condemn their demand as wicked? What does this reveal about their heart attitude and their failure to recognize the inherent authority of His words and deeds?

2. **Drawing Parallels:** With Jonah 3 as our backdrop, how does Jesus compare Himself to Jonah? What parallels does He draw between the faithless Jews demanding a sign and the Ninevites who responded to Jonah's simple proclamation of judgment? What does this reveal about the receptivity of the Gentiles versus the resistance of the Jews?

3. **Resisting the Sign:** Throughout Acts, we read of Jews resisting the inclusion of Gentiles by grace (i.e. 13:44–52; 15:1–5, 11;). Even with Jonah as a backdrop, why do you think the Jews resisted the grace of God going to Gentiles?

4. **Unveiling the Mystery:** Ephesians 2:11—3:13 sheds light on Gentile inclusion, referring to it as a "mystery" previously hidden but now revealed. How does this passage support and illuminate Jesus' use of "The Sign of Jonah" in Luke's Gospel?

5. **Peter's Transformation:** The early church grappled with the implications of Gentile salvation. In Acts 10:1–48, we witness Peter's initial reluctance to preach God's grace beyond the Jewish community. What were the foundations of his exclusionary mindset? How did God challenge and ultimately transform Peter's perspective, leading him to preach the Gospel to the Gentiles? And defend salvation by grace (Acts 15:6–11)?

6. **Empowered by Grace:** Reflect on your salvation as a Gentile. How should this profound reality empower you to share the Gospel with

others, recognizing that God's redemptive plan encompasses all nations and peoples?

A Broader Embrace

Luke's unique presentation of "The Sign of Jonah" broadens our understanding of Jesus' ministry and its implications for the world. By emphasizing the Gentiles' repentance, Luke foreshadows the radical inclusivity of the Gospel message, a theme that unfolds dramatically in the Book of Acts. This expanded perspective challenges us to recognize that God's salvation extends beyond cultural or ethnic boundaries, embracing all who respond in faith and repentance.

Prayer Prompt: Lord, thank you for the incredible gift of salvation through Jesus, a gift that extends to all people, regardless of their background or ethnicity. Help me to never take for granted the grace that has been shown to me, a Gentile, and to always appreciate the rich diversity of Your Kingdom.

Lesson 12

Paul: A Better Jonah

As Luke concludes the Book of Acts, he dedicates an unusually long passage to Paul's dramatic sea voyage to Rome. This extended narrative, filled with storms, shipwrecks, and surprising encounters, is more than just a travelogue. It's a deliberate echo of Jonah's story, designed to showcase Paul, the apostle to the Gentiles (Romans 11:13), as a "better Jonah," a man who embodies the true spirit of a servant of God. While Jonah ran from God's call to Nineveh, Paul willingly embraces his call (Act 23:11; 25:10–12) and journey to Rome, the heart of the empire that persecutes his people—to preach the message of salvation through Jesus Christ.

Before we embark on this comparative journey, let's set sail with Paul and experience the gripping events of Acts 27:1—28:31.

Navigating the Storms of Life and Faith

Now, let's explore the parallels between Jonah and Paul, drawing insights for our own lives:

1. **Prophet vs. Apostle:** Compile a comprehensive list of similarities and differences between Jonah and Paul's respective voyages. How do these comparisons illuminate their contrasting approaches to obedience, adversity, and proclaiming God's message?

2. **A Seasoned Sailor:** This was not Paul's first encounter with a shipwreck (cf. 2 Corinthians 11:25). How do you envision him and

his companions navigating the perils of the storm and the ensuing shipwreck? What qualities of leadership and resilience do they exhibit in the face of danger?

3. **Witnesses in Adversity:** Imagine being on that ship, facing a raging storm and imminent shipwreck. How is Paul's calm demeanor and confident words affecting you? How does his response to the crisis differ from the indifference of Jonah or the despair we often see during a crisis?

4. **Our Response to Storms:** Reflect on your reactions to life's inevitable trials. Do your responses draw others closer to God or inadvertently push them away? How can you cultivate a steadfast faith that inspires hope and confidence in those around you, even amidst adversity?

5. **A Captive Audience:** Drawing upon Paul's eloquent speeches in Acts 17:22–31 and 26:1–23, reconstruct the message you believe he proclaims to Caesar and the Roman court during his inevitable appearance before them. In what ways do you see him tailoring his message to this unique audience, presenting both judgment and grace with boldness and sensitivity?

6. **Embracing the Call:** As you actively proclaim the Gospel with those who are lost, reflect on how you can embody the qualities of a "better Jonah" (cf. 1 Corinthians 11:1). How can you demonstrate unwavering obedience, compassionate outreach, and a steadfast

commitment to proclaiming God's message, even in the face of opposition or adversity?

A Beacon of Hope in the Tempest

As we conclude our exploration of Paul's transformative journey, we recognize him as a "better Jonah," a shining example of hope and resilience amidst life's tempests. Like Jonah, Paul faced trials and tribulations, yet his unwavering faith and dedication to sharing the Gospel transformed those around him. His story inspires us to embrace our calling as ambassadors for Christ, reaching out to those around us and sharing the message of salvation, even in the face of adversity. By embodying the qualities of a "better Jonah," we can illuminate the path toward God's grace and inspire others to join us on this extraordinary journey of faith.

Prayer Prompt: Lord, open my eyes to see the needs of those around me, and give me a compassionate heart to reach out to them, just as Paul did on the ship. May my words and actions reflect Your love and grace, drawing others closer to You, even during the storms of life.

A Note from Clay

It's only right that I thank those who helped me write this book. First, I'm grateful to the Jackson Heights Church of Christ for allowing me to dedicate my life to the preaching and teaching of God's word. I'm especially thankful for the adults and high schoolers who endured the first edition of this book. Y'all really helped me work the kinks out of these studies.

I would be amiss if I didn't also thank my wife Shelly, for her unwavering support and encouragement throughout this process, especially for allowing me to work late into the night on these lessons. She has been a constant source of inspiration, and I couldn't have completed this study, let alone be the preacher I am, without her.

And thank you for working through this study with me. Jonah is a fascinating book that offers a wealth of insights into human nature, faith, and the transformative power of God's grace. As we delved into Jonah's story, we explored themes of disobedience, repentance, and the importance of sharing God's grace, even when it's difficult.

So let me leave you with this exhortation: Go forth from this study, not as reluctant, hesitant disciples, but as bold ambassadors of Christ, ready to proclaim His message of salvation, even in the face of adversity. Extend His grace to those around you, just as He has extended His grace to you. And never forget that God's love knows no bounds; it reaches beyond borders, cultures, and even our own understanding.

I hope that this book has been a valuable resource for you and that it has deepened your understanding of God's Word and His love for us. If this study has helped you, or if you have spiritual questions, I'd love to hear from you. Drop me a line at *clay@thebibleway.org* or if you're ever in the Columbia, Tennessee, area let's grab a cup of coffee and talk about our Jonah, Jesus, or Paul (and maybe a little Elvis, too!).

Thank you again for your participation in this study. May God bless you abundantly.

P.S. If you enjoyed this study, please consider sharing it with your friends and family. Together, we can spread the message of God's love and hope to the world.

Clay's Bio

Clay Gentry is the preacher at the Jackson Heights Church of Christ in Columbia, Tennessee. He shares his life with his wife of 25 years, Shelly, a reading specialist at Columbia Academy, and their four children: Isaac, Lillie, Micah, and Anna. When he's not in the pulpit, you might find him exploring an old cemetery, hiking scenic trails, repairing a car or two, or simply relaxing with a good book and a cup of coffee. *(He's also a huge Elvis fan, and secretly believes he can channel The King while singing karaoke. But that's a story for another time.)*